Cooking is My Therapy

Chef Kashia Zollicoffer

Pink Kiss Publishing Company
Biloxi, Mississippi

ISBN 978-0-9895580-0-6

Library of Congress Control Number: 2015935594

Published by:

Pink Kiss Publishing Company
296 Beauvoir, Rd., Suite 100-317
Biloxi, Mississippi 39531
(228) 366-6829
www.pinkkisspublishing.com

Cover designed by: Donna Osborn Clark
Interior designed by: Glenda A. Wallace

Contents

Introduction

For many years, cooking has been my passion. Since a little girl growing up in Carthage, Mississippi, I always enjoyed cooking in the kitchen and helping my grandmother. We would prepare food for all types of events, you name it, and we were there bringing delicious meals.

Approaching college, I could not figure out what I wanted to do with my life. Did I want to be a nurse, teacher or lawyer? I wanted to help people and I loved to entertain so I knew I wanted to reach people, but in what way? During my freshman year is where cooking became my therapy. Being away from my grandmother's hot meals to eating fast foods was devastating! I began to cook for myself and my fellow roommates. This is when I knew I wanted to become a cook and share my unique style of flavors and recipes.

After becoming a top 6 finalist on Season 12 of the Hit Series *Hell's Kitchen* I began to focus on different types of gourmet appetizers, meals, and desserts. Each one of these recipes was inspired by different experiences in my life. I hope you enjoy and thanks to everyone for their influences and continuous support!
Much Love,

Kashia Zollicoffer

New York Strip w/ Blue Cheese Crab Butter

Served with Roasted Asparagus

Ingredients:

2 8oz to 10oz New York Strips

5 - 6 tablespoons of blue cheese (Roquefort)

5 – 6 tablespoons butter

1 tablespoon finely chopped parsley

1 cup cooked crab meat

1 bunch asparagus, tough ends trimmed, rinsed and patted dry

6 tablespoons olive oil

1/2 tablespoons minced garlic

1 tablespoon of Salt

1 tablespoon ground black pepper

1 teaspoon fresh lemon juice

Material Needed:

Iron Skillet or Non Stick Skillet

Baking pan

Cutting board

Knife

Prep bowl

Directions

Preheat the oven to 425 degrees F.

In a large glass baking dish, toss the asparagus with the olive oil and garlic. Season lightly with salt and pepper, and toss. Bake until the asparagus are tender and lightly browned, 15 to 20 minutes, depending upon the thickness of the stalks, stirring twice.

Remove from the oven and toss with the lemon juice. Adjust the seasoning, to taste.

Serve warm or at room temperature.

Making New York Strip with Blue Cheese Crab Butter

While I do this recipe on the stove top, it is easily transferred to the grill.

In a bowl, mix the butter, crab, cheese and parsley together; it will be easier if they are at room temperature. Preheat oven to 450 degrees. Bring the steaks up to room temperature; season with salt and pepper Heat a frying pan (preferably a heavy bottom one) until it starts lightly smoking. Lay the New York Strips down and sear on one side for 3 – 5 minutes (depending on thickness and the desired doneness). Once crusty on one side, turn the steaks over and cook for 1 – 2 minutes. Slather the blue cheese butter onto both steaks, and transfer them to the oven for another 2 – 4 minutes until they are at the desired temperature. Remove the steaks from the oven and let them rest for about 5 minutes.

Saucy Tenderloin with Polenta

Ingredients:

1 ⅓ cups water
¼ teaspoon salt
1 can of chicken broth
1 cup yellow cornmeal
¾ beef tenderloin
Vegetable cooking spray
1 teaspoon olive oil
¼ teaspoon ground pepper
3 gloves garlic; mined
1 package fresh mushrooms; sliced
¼ minced shallots
¼ cup dry red wine
1 can of stewed tomatoes; undrained
1 tablespoon tomato paste
1 tablespoon chopped fresh thyme

Combine first three ingredients in a medium saucepan; bring to a boil. Add cornmeal in a slow, steady stream, stirring constantly. Reduce heat to medium, and cook, stirring constantly, 20 minutes or until cornmeal mixture (polenta) pulls away from sides of pan. Cut tenderloin into ¾ inch pieces, remember to trim fat. Coat a nonstick skillet with cooking spray; add oil. Place over medium-high heat until hot. Add meat, pepper and garlic; cook 4 minutes or until meat is browned on all sides, stirring often. Remove from skillet. Drain and pat dry. Wipe drippings from skillet.

Coat skillet and cooking spray; place over medium-high heat until hot. Add mushrooms and shallots; sauté 2 minutes. Add wine and tomatoes; bring to a boil. Reduce heat; simmer, uncovered, 5 minutes. Stir in tomato paste and thyme; simmer 3 minutes, stirring occasionally. Return meat mixture to skillet, and cook until thoroughly heated. When ready to serve, place meat mixture over polenta.

Makes 4 servings.

Ribeye with Shrimp Croquettes

Ingredients:

2 Ribeye Steaks
4 tablespoons of olive oil
Salt
Fresh ground black pepper
3 cloves garlic, minced
3 sprigs fresh thyme

Directions

Take your ribeye out of the refrigerator 20 minutes before if they are not room temperature Preheat oven to 350 degrees F. Heat olive oil in a cast iron skillet over high heat. Season each ribeye with salt and pepper. Make sure your grease is extremely hot. Began searing your ribeye until brown and crispy, about 3 minutes each side. Turn heat down to medium and fresh garlic, thyme and onions (optional) and add 3 tablespoons of butter. Using a tablespoon, baste the steaks with the melted butter mixture. Place your skillet in the oven for 4-6 minutes for medium rare, 8-10 for medium or longer for desired temperatures. Let rest for 3 minutes before serving.

Shrimp Croquettes

Ingredients:

2 cups shrimp, chopped
1 teaspoon parsley, minced
2 tablespoons lemon juice
¼ teaspoon salt
1/8 teaspoon cayenne pepper
1 pinch nutmeg
3 eggs, well beaten
Breadcrumbs
Vegetable, for frying
4 tablespoons flour

Directions

In a large bowl, mix all the ingredients together, mixing each ingredient one at a time. Mixture should become thick (if needed, add crackers for more thickness). After each item is mixed, shape croquettes to desired shape. Cook in a cast iron skillet with olive oil on medium-high heat. Once extremely hot, add each shrimp croquette clockwise in the skillet, turning in the same order. Allow each side to brown before turning. If needed, place in the oven for 3 minutes at 400F.

Delicious with different types of steaks or served as an appetizer!

Smothered Oxtails

Ingredients:

2 pounds beef oxtails
1 glove garlic, mined
1 tablespoon salt
1 teaspoon pepper
1 teaspoon Cajun seasoning
1 teaspoon seasoning salt

Directions

Place oxtails, garlic, onions, 1 tablespoon salt, 1 teaspoon pepper, Cajun seasoning, and seasoning salt in a large heavy pot. Drizzle olive oil over ingredients and leave searing for 10 minutes, stirring constantly. Once you finish, fill with enough water to cover oxtails, and place over high heat. Bring to a boil. Cover, and reduce heat to medium. Cook for 2 ½ to 3 hours (depending on size of oxtails). Remove from heat, and add tomato juice, paste and mixed peppers. Season with additional salt, pepper, and garlic powder if needed. Leave on medium heat for 20 minutes, stirring constantly, until tomato juice thickens. Remove from heat.

Oxtails should be tender and are best served with yellow rice or seasoned rice.

Granny's Cream Pound Cake

<u>Ingredients:</u>

3 sticks of salted butter (softened)

3 ½ cups of sugar

6 eggs

3 cups of sifted Cake Flour

½ pint heavy whipping cream

½ tsp. hazelnut extract

½ of a vanilla bean

Preparation

Preheat oven to 325F. Spray desired cake pan with cooking spray and lightly flour. Sift 3 cups of cake flour, and then sit it to the side. Combine sugar and butter until creamy in large bowl. Alternate the eggs, one at a time make sure each is beaten well. Add flour and whipping cream throughout this process until each of the three ingredients are gone. Stir the ½ teaspoon of the hazelnut extract and ½ of the inside of the vanilla bean. Mix well.

Baking

Pour cake mixture into pan. For approximately 1 hour 15 minutes - 1 hour 30 minutes. You may use a tester in the middle of the cake to make sure the cake is done. Make sure tester (toothpick) comes out clean. Allow to cool for 10-15 minutes.

If desired, add Lemon Glaze

Lemon Glaze

Ingredients:

2 cups of sifted powdered sugar
3 tablespoons of squeezed lemon
½ stick of butter (melted)
2 tablespoons of heavy cream

Preparation

Combine powdered sugar and butter in medium size bowl. Stir in 2 tablespoons of heavy cream. If desired, add ½ of lemon extract or favorite flavor. Beat until smooth and creamy. If necessary, add more cream. Drizzle over favorite dessert or Granny's Cream Pound Cake.

Chef Kashia Zollicoffer

Mushroom Basil Turkey Burger

Ingredients:

2 eggs, beaten

2 cloves of garlic; minced

½ bunch of basil; chopped

2 ½ of ground turkey

Serves 8

Preparation

Preheat a cast iron skillet on medium high heat and lightly oil with olive oil. While your skillet is preheating, mix together eggs, garlic, mushrooms, basil and turkey in a large bowl until well combined. Form patties into 8 servings. Cook until no longer pink or until desired temperature.

Preferred Condiments

Roman Tomatoes

Red Onions

Desired Lettuce

Spicy Mayo

Ingredients:

½ cup of pure olive oil
½ cup of vegetable oil
1 large egg yolk at room temperature
1 tablespoon of distilled white vinegar
½ teaspoon of kosher salt
2 tablespoons of lemon juice
2 tablespoons of chopped cilantro
2 cloves of garlic, minced
1 teaspoon of ground cumin
1 teaspoon of paprika
½ teaspoon of cayenne pepper
2 sliced roasted jalapenos

Preparation

Combine the olive and vegetable oil in a bowl and set aside. Whisk the egg yolk, vinegar and ½ teaspoon of salt in another small bowl. Set the bowl with the egg yolk aside also in a level area. Stir in oil mixture very slowly, whisking constantly. The mixture will begin to thicken and continue to whisk until smooth. Add lemon juice, cilantro, garlic, cumin, paprika, cayenne pepper and roasted jalapenos. Make sure all ingredients are thoroughly mixed. Refrigerate until ready to serve.

Delicious with burgers and other appetizers.

Pork Medallions and Cajun Rice

1(¾) pork tenderloin
1 teaspoon Creole seasoning, divided
Vegetables cooking spray
½ cup finely chopped sweet red pepper
½ cup finely chopped green pepper
½ cup finely chopped carrot
½ cup finely chopped celery
½ finely chopped onion
2 gloves garlic; mined
1 cup long grained, uncooked
2 ¼ cups of beef broth
1 bay leaf
Chopped parsley (optional)
Hot sauce (optional)

Trim fat from tenderloin. Cut tenderloin crosswise into 1-inch thick slices. Place between 2 sheets of heavy duty plastic wrap; flatten to ½ thicknesses. Sprinkle with ½ teaspoon Creole seasoning. Coat a large nonstick skillet with cooking spray. Add pork; cook over medium-high heat 3 minutes on each side or until browned. Remove from skillet, and keep warm.

Coat skillet with vegetable cooking spray; place over medium heat hot. Add red pepper and next 5 ingredients; sauté 8 to 10 minutes or until tender. Add rice, stir well. Add beef broth, bay leaf, and remaining ½ teaspoon Creole seasoning; bring to a boil. Cover, reduce heat, and simmer 20 minutes or until rice is tender and liquid is absorbed.

Return pork to skillet; remove from heat. Cover and let stand 5 minutes before serving. Remove and discard bay leaf. If desired, sprinkle with parsley and serve with hot sauce.

Tee's White Chocolate Cake

Ingredients:

¼ pound of white chocolate; chopped
½ cup boiling water
1 cup butter, softened
2 cups sugar
4 eggs, separated
1 vanilla bean
2 ½ cups sifted cake flour
1 teaspoon baking soda
1 cup buttermilk

Preparation

Combine chocolate and water, stirring until chocolate melts; set aside. Cream butter; gradually add sugar, beaten well at medium speed of electric mixer. Add egg yolks, one at a time, beating well after each addition. Stir in chocolate mixture and vanilla.

Combine flour and soda; add to chocolate mixture alternately with buttermilk, beginning and ending with flour mixture. Beat egg whites (at room temperature) until stiff peaks form; fold into chocolate mixture.

Pour batter into 3 well greased and floured 9 inch round cake pans. Bake at 350 for 25 minutes or until a wooden pick inserted in center comes clean. Cool in pans 10 minutes; remove and cool completely on a wire rack. Spread coconut pecan frosting between layers on sides of cake.

Coconut Pecan Frosting

Ingredients:

1 cup of evaporated milk
1 ½ cups of sugar
¼ cup of real butter
4 eggs yolks
1 ½ cups of flaked coconut
1 ½ cups of chopped pecans
½ vanilla bean

Preparation

Combine first four ingredients in a heavy saucepan; bring to a boil and cook over medium heat for 12 minutes, stirring constantly. Add coconut, pecans and inside of vanilla; stir until cool and thick enough to spread.

*Serving enough for one 3 layer cake.

Chocolate Lovers Cheesecake

1½ cups of chocolate wafer crumbs
¼ teaspoon ground nutmeg
½ cups of butter, melted
2 (8-ounces) packages cream cheese; softened
¾ cup of sugar
3 eggs
1 (8-ounces) carton sour cream
6 (1-ounce) squares semisweet chocolate, melted
1 tablespoon plus ¾ teaspoon cocoa
1 vanilla bean
½ cup whipping cream, whipped
Chocolate curls (optional)
Chopped Almonds (optional)

Preparation

Combine first 3 ingredients, mixing well. Press mixture into bottom of a 9 inch spring form pan to chill. Beat cream cheese at low speed of an electric mixer until light and fluffy; gradually add sugar, mixing well. Add eggs, one at a time, beating well after each addition. Stir in sour cream, melted chocolate, cocoa and inside of the vanilla bean; mix well. Gently place whip cream and spoon into prepared pan.

Bake at 300F for one hour. Turn oven off; allow cheesecake to cool in oven 30 minutes. Open door, and allow cheesecake to cool in oven 30 minutes. Open door, and allow cheesecake to cool in oven an additional 30 minutes. Refrigerate 8 hours. Remove sides of spring form pan, and garnish with additional whipped cream, chocolate curls, almonds if desired.

Cajun Beef Stew

Ingredients:

¼ cup Caribbean Jerk marinade
2 pounds beef stew meat
6 red potatoes; cut into fourths
⅓ cup of all purpose flour
1 can of diced tomatoes, undrained
3 cups of chopped red, green and yellow bell pepper and onions
1 bag of mixed vegetables (16 ounce bag)

Preparation

Pour marinade over beef in covered glass or plastic dish; coat beef with marinade. Let stand for 30-45 minutes. Spray inside of 4 to 5 quarts slow cooker with cooking spray. Place potatoes in slow cooker. Mix flour and Cajun seasoning; toss with beef and marinade, coating well. Place beef and marinade on potatoes. Add tomatoes. Cover and cook on low heat setting 7 to 8 hours or until beef is tender. Stir in vegetables. Cover and cook on low heat setting 15 to 30 minutes longer or until vegetables are tender.

*Serves 4 to 6

Sausage Stuffed Bell Peppers

Ingredients:

6 colored bell peppers
1lb ground sausage
1 ½ cups cooked rice
½ onion; minced
1(15 ounce) can of tomato sauce
Salt and Ground Pepper as desired

Directions

Preheat oven to 375F. Bring a pot of water to a boil. Add bell peppers to the boiling water and cook until softened, 5 to 8 minutes; drained. Sauté ground sausage in a large skillet over medium-high heat, breaking into small pieces with a spatula as it cooks, until completely brown, 7 to 10 minutes. Drain and discard excess grease. Transfer browned sausage into a large bowl.

Combine rice, onion and half the tomato sauce with ground sausage. Season with salt and black pepper. Stuff cooked bell pepper with the ground sausage mixture. Place stuffed bell peppers in a baking dish. Pour water into baking dish to about 1 inch deep. Pour remaining tomato sauce over the peppers. Bake in preheated oven until heated through, about 30 minutes. Prepare to serve!

Buttermilk Fried Chicken

Ingredients:

1 (3 pound) chicken, cut into 8 pieces
3 cups buttermilk
Salt as desired
Vegetable oil
2 cups of self rising flour
½ teaspoon paprika
Freshly ground pepper as desired
¼ teaspoon garlic powder
½ cayenne pepper
1 pinch dried thyme

Directions

Season chicken with salt and black pepper. After seasoning, cover chicken with buttermilk in a resealable plastic bag or container. Add thyme, additional black pepper, salt, cayenne pepper, garlic to buttermilk mixture and stir well. Cover and refrigerate for one hour or overnight. When you're ready to cook the chicken, let it sit at room temperature in the marinade for 30 minutes. Pour oil into large, straight-sided frying pan or cast iron skillet. Heat over medium-low heat for about 15 minutes or test it by sprinkling flour in oil. If oil is hot enough, the flour will sizzle. Combine the remaining a salt, black pepper, pinch of cayenne and thyme in a bowl with flour.

When the oil is ready, remove parts of the chicken from the buttermilk, letting the excess drip off. Coat the chicken in the flour mixture, shaking off the excess. Lay each of the pieces in the oil, remember to be careful. Fry each piece until cooked through and golden brown, flipping halfway through, about 20 minutes. Cut a small slit down to the bone; the juices should run clear and there should be no pink at the bone. Place cooked pieces of chicken on a wire rack covered with paper towel. Repeat with the remaining chicken. Delicious with mac and cheese and roasted cabbage.

Roasted Cabbage

Ingredients:

1 large green cabbage, outer leaves removed
Olive oil
4 slices thick bacon
Salt
Ground Black Pepper
1 onion; sliced
Red peppers (optional)
1 stick of butter, sliced

Directions

Heat the oven to 380F. Cut the cabbage into quarters and slice the bottom of each quarter to an angle to remove the core. Cut each quarter in half again, this will make 8 wedges. Cut 8 pieces of aluminum foil to fit each cabbage wedge. Place each of the cabbage wedges on the foil and drizzle lightly with olive oil. Sprinkle with salt and pepper as desired. Wrap each cabbage wedge with the bacon slices and 1 piece of butter. Add red pepper if desired.

Roast for about 45 minutes, flipping the cabbage wedges once halfway through. If the cabbage is not tender and browned enough for taste, place back in the oven for additional time. No longer than increments of 5 minutes.

Serve hot. Recipe makes 8 servings.

Lobster Mac and Cheese

<u>Ingredients:</u>

1 ½ bread crumbs
2 pounds of lobster meat, cooked
½ nutmeg
½ ground black pepper
3 cups sharp cheddar cheese
1 cup shredded cheddar for topping
5 cups gruyere cheese (optional)

½ cup all-purpose flour
1 sticks of unsalted butter; sliced
1 quart milk
1 egg
1 pound elbow macaroni
Vegetable oil
Salt as desired

<u>Directions</u>

Preheat oven to 375 degrees.

Drizzle oil into large pot of boiling salt water. Add pasta and cook accordingly to the directions on the package. Drain well. In the meantime, heat milk in a small saucepan, but do not bring to a boil. In a large pot, melt stick of butter and add flour. Cool on low for about 2-3 minutes stirring constantly. Add hot milk and cook for a minute or until thickened and smooth. Take off the heat and add the gruyere and cheddar cheese, 1 tablespoon salt, black pepper, egg and nutmeg. Add your cooked lobster and macaroni and mix well. Place mixture in glass baking pan. Combine the bread crumbs and remaining two slices of butter (melted) and sprinkle on top. If there is extra lobsters sprinkle this also. Bake for 25-35 minutes or until the macaroni is browned on top.

This is one of my favorite recipes. I love seafood and I hope you enjoy!

BBQ Chicken Meatball Skewers

Ingredients:

1 lbs. ground chicken

½ onion, mined

⅓ panko bread crumbs

1 egg

½ cayenne pepper

2 tbsp. olive oil

1 cup of Honey BBQ Sauce

Ranch dressing

Mix first five ingredients with ½ tsp of each salt and black pepper; shape mixture into 1 inch balls. In a large cast iron cook meatballs with olive oil over medium heat until browned for 10 minutes. Stir in the BBQ sauce and cook for simmer for about 2 minutes. Thread 4 meatballs per skewer and serve with ranch dressing.

Jalapeno-Mozzarella-Stuffed Sliders

Recipe makes 12 Sliders
Prep: 30 mins
Grill: 20 mins

Ingredients

¾ cup freshly grated Parmesan cheese
½ cup snipped fresh basil (optional)
⅓ cup snipped oil-
Drained 3 cloves garlic, minced
½ teaspoon freshly ground black pepper
¼ teaspoon salt
1 ½ pounds ground beef
6 ounces fresh mozzarella cheese
2 Jalapenos, diced
12 Potato Rolls

Directions

1. In a large bowl, combine Parmesan cheese, basil (if desired), garlic, pepper, and salt. Add ground beef; mix well. Shape meat mixture into 24 ½ -inch-thick patties.

2. Cut mozzarella cheese into twelve ¼ -inch-thick slices. Place mozzarella cheese on the centers of twelve of the patties. Top with the remaining twelve patties; pinch edges together to seal.

3. For a charcoal grill, place patties on grill rack over drip pan. Test for medium heat. Cover and grill for 20 to 25 minutes or until done (160 degreesF),* turning patties once halfway through grilling.

Prepare to serve with your favorite condiments!

Chef Kashia's Ribeye Fajitas

Ingredients

1 pound of rib eye steak, cut into thin strips
2 oregano leaves
2 teaspoons of Chef Kashia's Steak Seasoning
1 tablespoon of olive oil
1 medium green bell pepper, cut into thin strips
1 red bell pepper

1 medium onion, thinly sliced
8 flour tortillas, (6-inch)
½ cup of Blue Cheese Crumbles

Directions

1. Toss steak slices with seasoning and oregano in medium bowl. Set aside. Heat oil in large skillet on medium-high heat. Add bell pepper and onion; cook and stir for 5 minutes. Remove vegetable mixture from skillet.

2. Stir rib eye mixture into skillet; cook and stir 5 minutes or until the steak is no longer pink. Return vegetable mixture to skillet; cook and stir 1 to 2 minutes or until heated through.

3. Fry tortillas in medium high heat with cooking oil on both sides.

4. Spoon the rib eye and vegetable mixture onto fried tortillas. Serve with assorted toppings, if needed.

Red Velvet Brownies

Ingredients

½ cup unsalted butter, melted
1 cup white sugar
¼ cup unsweetened cocoa powder
1 ounce red food coloring

1 teaspoon vanilla extract

1 teaspoon distilled white vinegar

¼ teaspoon salt

2 large eggs, slightly beaten

¾ cup all-purpose flour

1 (8 ounce) package cream cheese at room temperature

¼ cup white sugar

1 large egg

¼ teaspoon vanilla extract

Directions

1. Preheat oven to 350 degrees F. Grease an 8x8-inch baking pan.

2. Whisk melted butter with 1 cup sugar in a large mixing bowl; stir cocoa, red food coloring, 1 teaspoon vanilla extract, vinegar, and salt into butter mixture one at a time, mixing well after each addition to avoid lumps. Stir 2 eggs into mixture until thoroughly combined.

3. Stir flour into cocoa mixture just until combined; set aside 1/4 cup batter. Pour remaining batter into the prepared baking dish.

4. Beat cream cheese in a bowl, using an electric mixer on medium speed until light and fluffy; beat ¼ cup sugar, 1 egg, and ¼ teaspoon vanilla extract into cream cheese

until very well blended and only small lumps remain, 3 to 4 minutes.

5. Spoon cream cheese mixture in dollops over the batter in pan; gently smooth tops of dollops evenly with batter using a knife or offset spatula. Do not over mix. Drizzle reserved ¼ cup of batter over the dollops of cream cheese mixture. Drag a knife or skewer through the batter and cream cheese mixture to create swirls.

6. Bake in the preheated oven until a toothpick inserted into the center of the pan comes out clean, 30 to 35 minutes. Cool completely before cutting into bars; You may add candied pecans as a topping if desired.

Creamy Mushroom Gravy

Ingredients

2 cups beef broth
½ cup all-purpose flour
¾ pound mushrooms, diced
½ cup chopped green onions
½ cup butter

Directions

In a medium saucepan over medium heat, sauté onions and mushroom with butter. Combine broth and flour once the onions and mushrooms are finished cooking down. Cook, stirring constantly, until golden brown and thickened. Prepare to serve!

If needed, you can add a can of cream of mushrooms to cheat and make gravy thick. This is my favorite gravy and I use this on several meats such as chicken, beef or turkey.

Country Sweet Potato Pie

Ingredients:
1 (1 pound) sweet potato
½ cup butter, softened
1 cup white sugar
½ evaporated milk
3 eggs
½ teaspoon ground nutmeg
½ teaspoon ground cinnamon
1 teaspoon vanilla extract
1 (9 inch) unbaked pie crust

Making the Sweet Potato Pie

1. Boil the sweet potato whole in skin for 40 to 50 minutes, or until done. Run cold water over the sweet potato, and remove the skin.

2. Break apart sweet potato in a bowl. Add butter, and mix well with mixer. Stir in sugar, milk, eggs, nutmeg, cinnamon and vanilla. Beat on medium speed until mixture is smooth. Pour filling into an unbaked pie crust.

3. Bake at 350 degrees F (175 degrees C) for 55 to 60 minutes, or until knife inserted in center comes out clean. Pie will puff up like a soufflé, and then will sink down as it cools.

Prepare to serve!

Chicken Stuffed with Spinach & Goat Cheese and Rice

Ingredients (for 2 - 3 servings)

2 boneless, skinless chicken breasts (normal cut, not strips or anything like that)

½ cups of baby spinach

½ cups of goat cheese

Olive oil

½ tablespoon salt

½ tablespoon ground black pepper

¼ cup butter

1 cup of rice

<u>Making the Stuffed Chicken:</u>

Heat a sauté pan over medium heat and add the spinach; season with salt and pepper. Toss the spinach until wilted; with should only take 3 – 4 minutes. Remove the spinach to a bowl and let it cool. While cooling, make the pocket in the chicken using a small paring knife. Hold the knife horizontal, and insert (with a stabbing motion) into the thickest part of the breast. Now swivel the tip of the knife, slowly expanding the pocket while keeping the base steady. That will keep the hole the same size, while creating the pocket. Once cooled, add the grated cheese to the sautéed spinach, mix and taste. Re-season if needed using about a teaspoon of stuffing at a time, fill the pockets in the chicken breasts, move the stuffing throughout the pocket as you go. Heat your oven to 375 degrees and bring a sauté pan to temperature over medium high heat. Season the outside of the stuffed chicken with salt and pepper. Add a few tablespoons of olive oil to the hot pan, and add the stuffed chicken breasts to sear. If you happen to tear a hole in the chicken, put the side with the hole in the pan first. Allow the chicken to sear for 3 – 4 minutes, before turning it over to sear on the other side for 3 – 4 minutes. Put the whole pan into the oven for another 5 – 8 minutes; until the chicken is cooked through; use a meat thermometer if you're in doubt. Make sure to allow the chicken to rest for a few minutes, or the stuffing will ooze out when cut. After resting, slice on the bias, and serve with the stuffing face up for a great presentation

<u>Material Needed</u>:

Saute Pan
Wooden Spoon
Cutting Board
Knife
Nonstick skillet

Honey Roasted Sweet Potatoes

Ingredients:
3 lbs sweet potatoes, peeled and cut into 3-in pieces
1 red chili pepper, seeded and thinly sliced
1 2-in piece fresh ginger, peeled and coarsely grated
4 tablespoons olive oil
¾ salt and black pepper as desired
3 tablespoons honey

Heat oven to 400F. On a large baking sheet, toss sweet potatoes, chili, ginger with oil, ¾ teaspoon of salt and pepper. Transfer half the potatoes to a second baking sheet. Roast both sides until sweet potatoes are golden brown and tender, 35 to 45 minutes. Remove from oven, drizzle the honey over the sweet potatoes and toss to combine.

Serve as an appetizer, with a steak or a yummy burger!

Classic Lasagna

Ingredients:
1 pound ground beef
2 jars (24oz) desired, tomato sauce
4 cups shredded mozzarella cheese
 4 cups ricotta cheese
12 lasagna noodles
½ cup grated Parmesan cheese
2 cloves garlic, chopped
1 teaspoon dried oregano
2 tablespoons olive oil
1 large egg

1 onion, chopped
1 green bell pepper, chopped
½ teaspoon of salt
½ ground black pepper

Directions

Cook pasta according to package instructions. In a saucepan, sauté ground beef with salt and black pepper, crumbling with a spoon until no longer pink. Add onion, bell pepper and garlic and sauté for 4 minutes. Add pasta sauce and set aside. In a bowl, blend ricotta cheese, egg, ¼ cup Parmesan cheese and 1 cup of mozzarella; set aside. Coat a 9/13 baking dish with olive oil and spread 1 cup of sauce at the bottom. Top with 3 lasagna noodles. Spread ¼ of the ricotta cheese mixture on the noodles and layer on 1 cup of the sauce mixture. Sprinkle ½ cup of mozzarella cheese on top. Repeat the process three times starting with noodles and finishing with remaining ¼ cup of Parmesan cheese. Sprinkle with oregano. Preheat oven to 350 degrees F and bake for 45 minutes until hot and bubbly. Let stand 10 minutes before cutting.

Best served with cheese biscuits.

Cheese Biscuits

Ingredients:

1 ½ cups all purpose flour

2 teaspoons baking powder

½ teaspoon baking soda

¼ teaspoon salt

¼ cup shredded cheese

1 vegetable oil

1 (8-ounce) carton plain yogurt

Vegetable spray

53

Directions

Combine first 4 ingredients in a bowl; make a well in center of mixture. Combine cheese and next 3 ingredients; add to flour mixture, stirring just until dry ingredient are moistened. Drop dough by 1/3 cupfuls, 2 inches apart, onto a baking sheet coated with cooking spray. Bake at 400F for 13 to 15 minutes or until golden. Serving makes 6.

Creamy Pecan Pie

Ingredients:

1 cup light corn syrup
3 eggs
1 ½ cup sugar
3 tablespoons butter; melted
2 cups of pecans
1 pie crust (your choice)
1 pack Philadelphia Sour cream (8 ounce)
1 teaspoon vanilla extract

Directions

Preheat oven to 375°F. Sour cream should already be at room temperature. In a large bowl, mix corn syrup, eggs, sugar, butter, sour cream and vanilla using a mixer or spoon. Pour filling into pie crust. You can neatly place the pecan on your mixture or stir in pecans (before pouring mixture into crust). Bake on center rack of oven for 46 to 60 minutes or until golden brown. Cool for 1 hour before serving.

Recipe makes 8-10 serving.

Fried Oreos

Ingredients:

2 cups milk
2 eggs
2 cups flour
1 teaspoon baking powder
½ salt
1 tablespoon sugar
1 package Oreo cookies (large)
Powdered sugar for coating

Directions

Preheat deep fryer to 375°F. In large bowl, mix the milk and eggs. In another bowl, sift together flour, baking powder, salt and sugar. Combine with the milk mixture. Beat to make smooth batter.

Using tongs or a fork, dip Oreos into the batter and let excess drip off. Carefully place in deep fryer, a few at a time. Cookies take about a minute or so to cook; turn gently to make sure both sides turn a light golden brown. When done, carefully remove with slotted spoon and place on paper-towel-lined tray to remove excess oil. Put cookies, a few at a time in a bowl or small bag of powdered sugar, shake gently. Serve warm with vanilla ice cream and caramel drizzle.

The Grandkid's Favorite Cornbread

Ingredients:

1 ½ cups cornmeal

3 cups all-purpose flour

1 ¼ cups sugar

2 Tablespoons baking powder

1 teaspoon salt

⅔ cup vegetable oil

⅓ cup butter, melted

2 Tablespoons honey

3 large eggs,

2½ cups whole milk

1 tablespoon of real mayonnaise

Preparation

Preheat oven to 375 degrees and grease a cast iron skillet (Place skillet in oven to preheat). In a large mixing bowl, stir the cornmeal, flour, sugar, baking powder, and salt. Pour in the vegetable oil, melted butter, honey, eggs, mayonnaise and milk, and stir just until moistened. Do not be afraid to add water if needed. Pour the batter into the greased cast iron skillet and bake in 375 degree oven for 35 minutes. Make sure to watch the cornbread towards the end. You want your cornbread to become golden brown or browned as desired. After removing from oven, serve warm with some delicious collard greens and honey glazed sweet potatoes!

Country Collard Greens

Ingredients:

½ pound ham hocks (can substitute with bacon)
2 red peppers
1 tablespoon of seasoned salt
2 large bunches of collard greens
½ cup vegetable oil
4 cups of salt
2 tablespoons black pepper

Directions

In a large pot, bring about 3-4 quarts of water to a boil with ham hocks (can substitute ham hocks with bacon), seasoned salt, half of the salt requested, black pepper and red peppers. Reduce heat to a medium-high and cook for 1 hour. Get the two bunches of collard and remove the stem that runs down the center. The heart of the collard, which is the leaves, does not need to be stripped. Stack 6 to 8 leaves on top of each other, roll up and slice into ½ to 1 inch thick slices. Wash the collards thoroughly. Place greens in pot with meat and vegetable oil. Cook for 45 to 60 minutes or until tender. Stir occasionally. When finished, taste and adjust seasoning.

Recipe makes 10-12 servings.

Enjoy!

About the Author

K ashia Zollicoffer is a self-taught culinary artist from Carthage, Mississippi. Growing up in a family steeped in culinary tradition, Kashia was exposed to a wide range of culinary cooking techniques at an early age. Many of her first vivid memories came from watching her mother cooking, catering events and those "Down South" family gatherings! By the time she was six, she can recall helping in the kitchen, and this is where her passion begun.

Although she has never taken a culinary class, Kashia takes her career just as seriously! When she decided to perfect her passion for food, she studied recipes, watched YouTube videos and absorbed many techniques from her idols, such as Paula Deen, Gordon Ramsey, and Rachael Ray. This also helped motivate her career because her idols were also self-taught.

After high school, Kashia was accepted to Jackson State University with a major in Special Education. While attending college, she would take advantage of any cooking opportunity given. Kashia catered jobs and gave numerous samples to classmates or anyone in need of food. She enjoyed feeding people and watching how much they enjoyed her work.

By 2010, Kashia decided to step out on faith and focus on the only career that seemed destined for her... COOKING! She moved to Atlanta, Georgia to study diverse dining cultures, different spices in hopes of attending culinary school. However, things did not go as planned and she had to relocate back to Mississippi. Where some would have given up, she worked even harder to perfect her craft, travel, share her talents and working closer toward her goals.

After returning home, Kashia auditioned for FOX hit television show, *Hell's Kitchen*, She became one of the top contestants of Season 12, finishing with a black jacket in the top 6 from Chef Ramsey.

Determined to be a notable role model and leader, Kashia stays active in her community as well as her personal life. She coordinates events, private catering and cooking for local shelters. Kashia's latest endeavors have led to her opening her own restaurant "Urban Country Kitchen" in Walnut Grove, Mississippi. You can find this Southern Belle having a great time, taking care of business, enjoying life and making her dreams come true daily. She encourages other that you can be anything with hard work and dedication!

If you would like more information about *Chef Kashia Zollicoffer* or *Cooking is My Therapy,* or to schedule an interview, please contact Pink Kiss Publishing Company at (228) 366-6829 or by e-mail at sales@pinkkisspublishing.com.

You can also email the Chef Kashia directly at: kashiazollicoffer@gmail.com.

For upcoming events and signings, please visit: pinkkisspublishing.com/ChefKashia.html

Notes

Use this section to make notes, modify recipes, or create your own recipes. Feel free to be creative!

And remember: **Cooking is My Therapy! It could be yours, too!**

Don't hold back, there's PLENTY of space. 😄

She really left a lot of space for notes, huh!?

Interested in joining our Pink Kiss Publishing family? Visit our website for more details!

www.pinkkisspublishing.com

Pink Kiss Publishing Company
Attn: Glenda A. Wallace/CEO
glendawallace@pinkkisspublishing.com
296 Beauvoir Rd, Suite 100-317
Biloxi, MS 39531
228-366-6829 /Office
228-205-3610 /Fax

Some more blank pages...

Maybe use this area to draw whatever comes to mind right after eating a particularly delicious meal and you're feeling relaxed and happy :)

This page looks like the perfect spot to jot down a few song lyrics!

Hmm. You're call here.

Ans here.

Here's a prompt.

Draw the first animal
  that comes to mind: _____
                       animal

Eating the first food
  that comes to mind: _____
                       food

Send me a pic!!
          ⌣

Feeling flustrated?
Sounds like a good time to
keep it simple with grilled cheese
and Chikerina soup. Can't beat a classic!

CPSIA information can be obtained
at www.ICGtesting.com
Printed in the USA
BVHW092022030121
596836BV00003B/169